Healthy Popsicle Recipes

Discover Delicious and Creative Ideas for Sharing in the Warm Weather

Healthy Popsicle Recipes

BookSumo Press
All rights reserved

Published by:
http://www.booksumo.com

Table of Contents

Introduction to Popsicles

Welcome to the cool, colorful world of popsicles—a frozen delight that transcends generations and brings a burst of joy with every lick. Popsicles tantalize taste buds offer respite from the sweltering heat, and have become a universal symbol of refreshment and joy. In this introductory chapter, we embark on a journey into the cool and colorful world of popsicles, exploring the diverse forms, flavors, and the sheer creativity that defines these icy confections.

At its core, a popsicle is a frozen dessert on a stick—a simple yet ingenious concept that has captivated generations. This chapter aims to unravel the essence of popsicles, examining the key components that make them a cherished favorite among people of all ages. From the iconic fruit pops to the creamy indulgence of dairy-based varieties, popsicles showcase an incredible versatility that contributes to their widespread appeal.

Popsicles are not just frozen treats; they are cultural phenomena that reflect the vibrant spirit of innovation in the culinary world. This section explores the dynamic landscape of popsicle culture, where experimental flavors, artistic presentations, and even gourmet renditions have elevated the humble popsicle to a form of edible art. The chapter delves into current trends, including the rise of artisanal popsicle shops, the influence of social media on popsicle aesthetics, and the ever-evolving spectrum of flavors that cater to an increasingly diverse palate.

Beyond taste, popsicles are a feast for the eyes. This section delves into the artistry involved in crafting visually appealing popsicles. From vibrant fruit layers to intricately swirled patterns, popsicle aesthetics play a crucial role in enhancing the overall experience. Popsicles come in various forms, each catering to different preferences and occasions. Whether it's the classic single-flavor popsicle, the multi-layered and adventurous rainbow pops, or the sophisticated and creamy gourmet pops, this section sheds light on the diverse formats that popsicles can take. From choosing the right molds to experimenting with flavors, it encourages readers to embrace the creativity that comes with homemade popsicle-making. In this book, we set the stage for a comprehensive exploration of popsicles, laying the foundation for a delightful journey into the realm of frozen confections that transcend seasons and bring joy with every lick.

A Love Affair for Popsicles

In the heat of summer's embrace, where the sun dances high and the air shimmers with warmth, there emerges a love affair that transcends generations—the enchanting world of popsicles. The mere sight of those familiar colors can transport you to a simpler time—of carefree afternoons and the thrill of chasing down the ice cream truck. Popsicles are not just frozen treats; they are time machines that whisk us back to the days of innocence, sparking memories that linger with each sweet bite. Beyond their frozen allure, popsicles have become cultural symbols deeply ingrained in diverse traditions. In this section, we unravel the threads of cultural significance woven into popsicles. From being staples of summer festivals to the sweet notes of celebration, explore how popsicles have become more than a treat—they are embodiments of cultural identity and shared experiences.

Picture a scene—a neighborhood block party, children's laughter echoing in the air, and the communal delight of shared popsicles. Popsicles have an innate ability to bring people together, creating shared moments of joy and connection. This segment celebrates the social aspect of popsicle enjoyment, emphasizing the delight they bring to gatherings and the sense of community they foster.

Embark on this delicious journey through "A Love Affair for Popsicles," where vibrant memories, cultural richness, and shared joy converge into a symphony of frozen delight. This chapter celebrates the irresistible charm of popsicles, inviting you to savor every moment of this love affair with frozen sweetness.

Rediscovering the Joy of Popsicles

A kaleidoscope of colors, inventive flavors, and a resurgence of enthusiasm for the frozen wonders we fondly call popsicles. As we delve into the heart of popsicles, prepare to be captivated by the culinary renaissance that has taken popsicles from nostalgic treats to gastronomic masterpieces. It's a revival that transcends generations, reigniting the passion for these frozen delights. Buckle up for a taste bud expedition as we unravel the innovative tapestry of popsicle flavors. From exotic fruit blends to unexpected savory twists, the popsicle landscape has expanded far beyond its traditional boundaries.

Rediscover the joy of savoring popsicles as artisanal treasures, each bite a testament to the dedication of those who craft these frozen delights. From the streets of Tokyo to the beaches of Rio de Janeiro, explore how popsicles have become cultural canvases, reflecting the diversity of global taste. The joy of popsicles extends beyond mere indulgence; it can be a guilt-free pleasure that aligns with wellness goals. From refreshing fruit pops to nutrient-packed creations, discover how popsicles are evolving to cater to health-conscious enthusiasts without compromising on the delightful experience.

As we delve into the world of popsicles, from their resurgence in culinary circles to their diverse cultural adaptations, from artisanal craftsmanship to their evolving role in our pursuit of wellness. It is an invitation to savor the frozen delights that have stood the test of time and continue to bring boundless joy with each lick and slurp.

Historical Evolution of Popsicles

The popsicle, a beloved frozen treat, has an intriguing history that spans over a century. Its evolution reflects not only advancements in refrigeration technology but also the creative spirit of those who sought to bring frozen joy to the masses.

The popsicle's story begins in the early 20th century with an accidental invention. In 1905, 11-year-old Frank Epperson left a mixture of soda and water with a stirring stick on his porch overnight. The result? A frozen delight he named the "Epsicle." This serendipitous incident laid the foundation for the icy treats we enjoy today.

Recognizing the potential, Epperson patented his creation in 1924. However, it was during the Great Depression that the popsicle gained widespread popularity. Street vendors sold them for just a nickel, providing an affordable and refreshing escape during challenging times. In 1923, Epperson introduced the concept at an amusement park, and by 1925, he began producing and selling "Epsicles." The brand evolved into what we now know as Popsicle. The name, a blend of "pop" and "icicle," captures the essence of this frozen treat's simplicity and joy.

As popsicles gained popularity, the range of flavors expanded. From the classic fruity options to creamy delights, the popsicle repertoire grew, catering to diverse tastes. The ability to experiment with flavors became a hallmark of the popsicle experience. Popsicles have been part of numerous cultural moments. From becoming a staple in the summer diet to being featured in artistic endeavors, the popsicle has transcended its humble origins to become a symbol of shared enjoyment and nostalgia.

The mid-20th century saw significant technological advancements, leading to the mass production and distribution of popsicles. Advances in refrigeration and packaging allowed for easy access, turning the popsicle into a household name. As travel and communication expanded, so did the popularity of popsicles worldwide. Each culture added its unique twist, introducing flavors and variations that reflected local tastes and traditions.

The 21st century brought about a renaissance in popsicle innovation. Gourmet popsicle shops emerged, offering artisanal flavors and premium ingredients. The popsicle's journey from a porch experiment to a global sensation is a testament to the enduring appeal of frozen delights. As we savor each icy bite, we pay homage to the inventors and innovators who transformed a simple frozen treat into a cultural icon.

Conversion Tables

DRY CONVERSIONS

Ounce (oz)	Tablespoon (tbsp)	US cup (c)	Grams (g)
1 oz	2 tbsp	⅛ c	28 g
2 oz	4 tbsp	¼ c	57 g
3 oz	6 tbsp	⅓ c	85 g
4 oz	8 tbsp	½ c	115 g or ¼ lb
8 oz	16 tbsp	1 c	227 g or ½ lb
16 oz	32 tbsp	2 c	455 g or 1 lb

WET CONVERSIONS

Fluid Ounce (fl. oz)	Tablespoon (tbsp)	US cup (c)	Milliliter (ml.)
1 fl. oz	2 tbsp	⅛ c	30 ml.
2 fl. oz	4 tbsp	¼ c	60 ml.
4 fl. oz	8 tbsp	½ c	120 ml.
8 fl. oz	16 tbsp	⅔ c	160 ml.
12 fl. oz	24 tbsp	¾ c	177 ml.
16 fl. oz	32 tbsp	1 c or ½ pint or ¼ quart	237 ml.

Understanding Popsicles

Popsicles, at their core, are a simple yet ingenious concoction. Born out of the need for a refreshing treat, their inception traces back to the early 20th century. As we unravel the threads of popsicles, we discover the creativity that led to the birth of this icy wonder and how it has evolved from a basic ice pop to a canvas of culinary innovation.

POPSICLES: IT'S NOT A ROCKET SCIENCE

But what makes a popsicle a popsicle? It's not rocket science, and in this section, we break down the fundamental components. From the base ingredients that create the icy texture to the myriad flavors that tantalize our taste buds, understanding the anatomy of a popsicle sets the stage for an appreciation of their versatility and universal appeal.

At the heart of a great popsicle lies the perfect blend of ingredients. We explore the role of fruits, juices, yogurts, and even unconventional additions that elevate popsicles from basic to extraordinary. Whether you're aiming for a classic fruit pop or a creamy indulgence, the key is in balancing flavors, sweetness, and texture.

TIPS AND TRICKS TO MAKE POPSICLES

Popsicle-making is an art form, and mastering the craft involves a blend of creativity, technique, and a dash of experimentation. In this chapter, we unravel the secrets and share expert tips and tricks to elevate your popsicle game, ensuring each frozen creation is a delightful masterpiece.

Flavor Fusion Mastery

Popsicles are a canvas for flavor exploration. Mix and match fruits, juices, and even herbs to create unique flavor profiles. Consider the interplay of sweet and tart, experiment with unexpected combinations, and balance the intensity of flavors for a harmonious taste experience.

The Perfect Texture

Achieving the ideal popsicle texture involves more than freezing fruit juice. Incorporating ingredients like yogurt, coconut milk, or pureed fruits can add creaminess and prevent your popsicles from becoming overly icy. Strike the right balance to ensure a satisfying, melt-in-the-mouth consistency.

Layering Techniques

Elevate the visual appeal of your popsicles through expert layering. Whether you're aiming for a rainbow effect or a sophisticated look, strategic layering adds aesthetic charm. Freeze each layer individually for crisp, defined boundaries that showcase your artistic flair.

Unleash the Garnish Power

Popsicles love a good garnish. Roll your creations in crushed nuts, dip them in chocolate, or sprinkle them with shredded coconut. The possibilities are endless. Garnishes not only enhance flavor but also add a delightful crunch and a touch of elegance.

Mindful Freezing

Patience is key in the popsicle-making process. Avoid the temptation to rush the freezing stage, as uneven freezing can result in icy textures. Allow ample time for each layer to set, ensuring a well-structured and visually appealing popsicle.

Incorporate Edible Surprises

Elevate your popsicles by incorporating hidden surprises. Embed chunks of fresh fruit, layer in unexpected fillings, or introduce a burst of flavor in the center. These edible surprises turn your popsicles into delightful treasures waiting to be discovered.

Creative Molds and Shapes

Break away from traditional molds and experiment with diverse shapes and sizes. Silicone molds offer flexibility, allowing you to craft popsicles that mimic your favorite objects or themes. Get playful and let your imagination run wild.

Temperature-Controlled Dipping

For those who enjoy a little extra indulgence, consider dipping your popsicles in chocolate or yogurt. Mastering the art of temperature control during the dipping process ensures a smooth, glossy coating that complements the frozen interior.

As you embark on your popsicle-making adventure, remember that each frozen creation is a reflection of your creativity. These tips and tricks serve as your guide to transforming simple ingredients into frozen masterpieces that delight the senses and bring joy with every bite. Let your imagination soar, and may your popsicles be as unique and wonderful as the moments you create while enjoying them.

The Basics of Popsicle Making

Popsicles, with their refreshing allure and vibrant colors, have become a universal symbol of summertime bliss. While store-bought options abound, there's a unique joy in creating your frozen treats at home. In this chapter, we delve into the essentials of popsicle making, unlocking the secrets to crafting icy delights that cater to your taste preferences and creative whims.

THE FOUNDATION OF DELECTABLE POPSICLES: INGREDIENTS

Embarking on the journey of creating popsicles is a delightful exploration of flavors, textures, and creativity. At the heart of this frozen symphony lie carefully selected ingredients that form the foundation of every delectable popsicle. Understanding the nuanced roles of these components is essential for crafting frozen treats that delight the palate.

Liquid Bases

The choice of liquid base is the canvas upon which the popsicle's flavor profile is painted. From the refreshing zing of fruit juices to the creamy indulgence of dairy and non-dairy options, each liquid base imparts a distinct character to the popsicle.

Fresh Juices

Fruit juices offer a burst of natural sweetness and vibrant flavors. Citrus juices bring a tangy kick, while berry juices contribute rich, fruity notes. The versatility of fruit juices allows for a spectrum of refreshing choices.

Dairy And Non-Dairy Options

The realm of liquid bases expands with dairy and non-dairy alternatives. These dairy-free options cater to individuals with lactose intolerance or those looking to explore a more exotic popsicle experience.

Whole Milk: Whole milk, with its rich and creamy consistency, serves as a classic base for popsicles. Its higher fat content contributes to a luscious mouthfeel, creating popsicles with a luxurious texture.

Cream: Cream, with its higher fat content than whole milk, elevates popsicles to a level of decadence. Adding cream results in a velvety texture and a more pronounced richness.

Yogurt: It introduces a tangy and refreshing dimension to popsicles, making it a popular choice for those seeking a lighter, more vibrant treat.

Coconut Milk: For those embracing dairy-free alternatives, coconut milk emerges as a star ingredient in popsicle making. Its velvety texture and tropical essence bring a unique twist to frozen treats.

Natural Sweeteners

Balancing sweetness is an art in popsicle making, and natural sweeteners add depth without overwhelming. From the golden richness of honey to the nuanced sweetness of maple syrup and the calorie-conscious sweetness of stevia, these natural sweeteners harmonize with other ingredients.

Honey: Honey, a natural sweetener with a distinct flavor profile, adds depth and complexity to popsicles. Its natural sweetness enhances the overall taste without overpowering other ingredients. With its ability to dissolve easily, honey blends seamlessly with liquid bases, ensuring a homogeneous sweetness throughout the popsicle.

Maple Syrup: Maple syrup's liquid consistency allows for easy incorporation into popsicle mixtures, ensuring even distribution of sweetness. Its distinctive caramel undertones provide a warm and comforting flavor, making it an excellent choice for autumn-inspired popsicles or those featuring ingredients like nuts and spices.

Stevia: Stevia, a plant-derived sweetener known for its intense sweetness with minimal calories, caters to individuals seeking a sugar-free or low-calorie popsicle option. Its concentrated sweetness requires only a small amount to achieve the desired level of sweetness.

Flavor Extracts

The world of popsicle making is a canvas of creativity where flavor extracts play the role of vibrant paint, transforming simple frozen treats into delightful masterpieces. Vanilla, mint, coffee, and chocolate syrup extracts each bring their unique charm to the popsicle-making process, opening doors to a myriad of taste experiences.

Vanilla Extract: Its warm, sweet, and comforting essence serves as a foundational flavor that complements a wide range of ingredients. Whether blended with fruity concoctions or swirled into creamy bases, vanilla extract introduces a classic and universally loved note to popsicles.

Mint Extracts: The cool and herbaceous notes of mint make it an ideal companion for fruit-based popsicles, adding a burst of freshness to the palate. Whether layered with citrus fruits or incorporated into creamy mixtures, mint extracts offer a versatile way to enhance the overall sensory appeal of popsicles.

Coffee Flavoring: For those who savor the bold and robust essence of coffee, coffee flavoring extracts offer a pathway to popsicle indulgence. Whether utilizing brewed coffee or concentrated extracts, the addition of coffee flavoring introduces a sophisticated and rich character to popsicles.

Chocolate Syrup: A decadent and delightful addition, chocolate syrup extracts infuse popsicles with the irresistible taste of chocolate. In liquid form, chocolate syrup seamlessly integrates into popsicle mixtures, creating a smooth and velvety texture.

Vegetables

The introduction of vegetables adds a refreshing and nutritious dimension to frozen delights. Vegetables bring their unique qualities, introducing vibrant colors, subtle sweetness, and additional nutritional benefits.

Cucumber: Cucumber, with its high water content and mild flavor contributes a hydrating and crisp element to popsicles. Paired with citrus fruits or mint, cucumber-infused popsicles offer a rejuvenating experience.

Avocado: Avocado, celebrated for its creamy texture and healthy fats, introduces a luscious and velvety quality to popsicles. When blended with tropical fruits or berries, avocado imparts a decadent and indulgent character, elevating the popsicle's richness.

Carrot: Carrots, known for their natural sweetness and vibrant orange hue, bring a touch of sweetness and earthiness to popsicles. Paired with fruits like pineapple or mango, carrot-infused popsicles strike a balance between sweetness and a subtle vegetable undertone.

Bell Peppers: Bell peppers, available in an array of colors, introduce a slightly tangy and crisp element to popsicles. Their sweetness pairs well with fruits like strawberries or peaches, creating popsicles that boast a delightful combination of flavors and textures.

Tomato: Tomato, often associated with savory dishes, takes a surprising turn in the popsicle realm. When combined with fruits like watermelon or strawberries, tomato brings a subtle sweetness and acidity, creating a popsicle with a nuanced flavor profile.

Add-Ins

While the foundation of popsicles relies on liquid bases, sweeteners, and flavor extracts, the addition of various textures enhances the overall experience. Add-ins, such as dried fruits, nuts, and sprinkles, introduce a delightful crunch, chewiness, or a burst of color to every icy bite.

Dried Fruits: Whether it's the chewiness of dried apricots, the intensity of raisins, or the tropical notes of dried pineapple, these additions bring bursts of concentrated flavor. Mixed into the popsicle base, dried fruits provide pockets of sweetness and a chewy texture.

Nuts: Nuts, with their crunch and richness, offer a satisfying contrast to the smoothness of popsicle bases. Almonds, walnuts, or pistachios can be finely chopped and stirred into the mixture, imparting a nutty flavor and a delightful crunch.

Sprinkles: Sprinkles, often associated with the whimsy of childhood treats, bring a burst of color and a playful element to popsicles. Whether they're classic rainbow sprinkles or themed shapes, sprinkles add a visual appeal that enhances the overall enjoyment.

In the realm of popsicle creation, these ingredients serve as the building blocks of endless possibilities, allowing enthusiasts to tailor frozen concoctions to their preferences and unleash their culinary imagination. Whether crafting a refreshing fruit medley or a decadent chocolate creation, the magic lies in understanding and artfully combining these components.

TOOLS OF TRADE FOR MAKING POPSICLES

Embarking on the journey of creating homemade popsicles is not only an art but also a science that requires a set of essential tools. These tools, each playing a unique role, ensure the seamless preparation and freezing of these frozen delights. From molds to garnishing tools, the right equipment transforms a simple frozen treat into a well-crafted popsicle masterpiece.

Popsicle Molds

At the heart of popsicle creation lies the popsicle mold. Brands like **Zoku** and **Norpro** offer molds in various shapes and sizes, allowing for the artistic expression of frozen treats. The mold's design dictates the final form of the popsicle, setting the stage for a visually appealing and delectable outcome.

Popsicle Sticks

Simple yet indispensable, popsicle sticks provide the handle and structure necessary for enjoying these frozen delights. Brands like **Wooden Craft Sticks** offer a classic option, while eco-friendly alternatives like bamboo sticks contribute to sustainable popsicle enjoyment.

Popsicle Holders

Popsicle holders, often silicone-based, offer a comfortable grip while enjoying frozen treats. Brands such as **Ozera** and **Kootek** provide options that not only insulate against the cold but also catch any drips, ensuring a mess-free experience.

Silicone Sleeves

Silicone sleeves act as insulating covers for popsicles, allowing for slower melting and more leisurely enjoyment. Brands like **Lekue** and **Peak Life** provide durable and reusable options, promoting a sustainable approach to popsicle creation.

Squeeze Bottles

Precision in pouring and layering is achieved with squeeze bottles, enabling controlled additions to popsicle molds. Brands such as **Belinlen** and **Squeeze Master** offer reliable options for the meticulous application of liquid ingredients.

Piping Bags

Piping bags, a staple in the world of pastry, find a place in popsicle creation. Brands like **Wilton** and **Ateco** provide options for neatly filling molds with various layers of flavored mixes, adding a professional touch to homemade popsicles.

Electric Blender

Achieving the perfect popsicle base requires the assistance of an electric blender. Brands like **Vitamix** and **Ninja** offer powerful blending options, ensuring a smooth and consistent mixture for freezing.

Measuring Cups

Precision in ingredient measurement is key to a successful popsicle. Brands like **Pyrex** and **OXO** provide reliable measuring cups, allowing for accurate portions of liquid bases and flavorings.

Microplane Zester

For those who seek to elevate their popsicles with zest and flavor, a microplane zester becomes a valuable tool. Brands like **Microplane** and **OXO** offer reliable options for grating citrus peels and adding bursts of freshness.

Measuring Spoons

Delicate flavor adjustments demand the precision of measuring spoons. Brands like **U-Taste** and **Prepworks** offer sets that ensure the accurate incorporation of spices and extracts.

Mesh Sieve

A mesh sieve becomes a refining tool in popsicle creation, ensuring a smooth base by eliminating unwanted pulp or seeds. Brands like **Cuisinart** and **OXO** provide durable options for this essential straining process.

Resealable Bags

In the world of popsicles, resealable bags become vessels for freezing, offering a convenient and space-efficient storage solution. Brands like **Ziploc** and **Hefty** provide reliable options for preserving popsicles until the perfect moment.

Airtight Freezer Containers

Preserving the integrity of popsicles in the freezer requires airtight containers. Brands like **Rubbermaid** and **OXO** provide containers that prevent freezer burn and maintain optimal freshness.

Spatula

A spatula becomes the tool of choice for effortlessly releasing popsicles from molds. Brands like **DI ORO** and **GIR** offer spatulas that ensure a smooth extraction without damaging the frozen treat.

Tongs

For a sanitary and efficient popsicle transfer from mold to the holder, tongs become invaluable. Brands like **OXO** and **Winco** offer options that maintain hygiene while handling these frozen delights.

Garnishing Tools

The final touch to a popsicle masterpiece often involves garnishing. Tools like garnishing tweezers and brushes, available from brands like **JB Prince** and **Ateco**, allow for precise decoration, turning each popsicle into a work of art.

The tools of the trade are more than mere utensils; they are the architects of frozen joy. With a thoughtful selection of molds, sticks, holders, and an array of precision tools, crafting popsicles transforms into a meticulous and delightful process, offering a frozen canvas for creative expression.

Easy Substitutions

While you're organizing your popsicle gathering, keep in mind your guests' preferences. Our cookbook features recipes tailored for those with specific dietary needs or health considerations, along with advice on how to adjust or remove ingredients to accommodate their requirements

Essential Ingredient	Substitution
Buttermilk	1 cup milk + 1 tbsp vinegar or lemon juice
Dairy Milk	1 cup nut milk (almond, soy, oat)
Nut Milk	1 cup dairy milk
Eggs	1 ripe banana mashed
Yogurt	1 cup buttermilk + 1 tbsp lemon juice
Sour Cream	1 cup plain Greek yogurt
Vanilla Extract	1 tsp almond extract
Granulated Sugar	1 cup coconut sugar or brown sugar
Brown Sugar	1 cup granulated sugar or coconut sugar
Butter	1 cup coconut oil or margarine
Oil	1 cup applesauce
Coconut Oil	1 cup vegetable oil
Salt	Kosher Salt
Chopped Nuts	Chopped seeds (sunflower, pumpkin) or dried fruits
Dried Fruits	Chopped nuts or chocolate chips
Chocolate Chips	Chopped nuts or dried fruits

How Easy Substitutions Are Important in Popsicle-Making?

The art of easy substitutions in popsicle-making not only introduces a world of innovation but also ensures that the magic of flipping popsicle is accessible to all, regardless of dietary preferences, restrictions, or ingredient availability. As we delve into the realm of popsicle and the profound impact of easy substitutions, we unearth a culinary treasure trove that celebrates diversity, experimentation, and the joy of breaking culinary boundaries.

1. A World of Flavorful Choices

Imagine a world where dietary restrictions or ingredient unavailability no longer inhibit the joy of popsicle creation. Easy substitutions invite us to transcend traditional recipes and embark on a culinary journey that embraces a multitude of ingredients and flavors. Be it substituting all-purpose flour with gluten-free alternatives, dairy milk with nut milk, or eggs with plant-based binders, the possibilities are as vast as the imaginations of the cooks themselves.

2. Catering to Health and Well-being

In an era where health-consciousness and dietary restrictions have become integral to our culinary landscape, easy substitutions play a pivotal role in fostering a sense of inclusivity. Whether due to allergies, sensitivities, or a conscious decision to adopt a certain dietary lifestyle, these substitutions allow everyone to indulge in the joy of popsicle without compromising on their well-being.

3. Empowering Creativity and Experimentation

The beauty of easy substitutions lies in their ability to awaken the inner chef and encourage culinary experimentation. With a dash of creativity, a sprinkle of curiosity, and a willingness to explore, popsicle-making becomes a canvas for innovation. Substituting vanilla extract with almond extract, incorporating mashed bananas for added sweetness, or infusing vibrant spices like cinnamon or cardamom can elevate a humble popsicle to a gourmet masterpiece.

4. A Sustainable Culinary Approach

As the world shifts its focus towards sustainability and mindful consumption, easy substitutions offer an environmentally conscious approach to popsicle-making. By opting for plant-based ingredients or utilizing readily available ingredients, we contribute to a sustainable food ecosystem.

5. Culinary Adventure and Adaptability

Just as life is a journey of constant change, so is the culinary world a realm of perpetual evolution. Easy substitutions celebrate this adaptability by allowing us to embrace unforeseen challenges with grace and creativity. When a certain ingredient is missing from our pantry or a dietary requirement arises unexpectedly, the art of substitutions ensures that our popsicle-making endeavor remains unfazed.

In the grand tapestry of cooking, easy substitutions in popsicle-making stand as a testament to the fluidity and universality of flavor. They remind us that culinary traditions are never set in stone; they're invitations to explore, experiment, and infuse our personal touch. As we navigate the culinary landscapes, may we carry with us the spirit of easy substitutions – a culinary compass that guides us towards a world of flavors, a world where dietary preferences are honored, and a world where popsicle transcend the ordinary to become extraordinary expressions of taste and ingenuity.

Popsicles Making Techniques

As the allure of popsicles extends beyond the realms of store-bought options, mastering the techniques becomes a rewarding endeavor. Each step, from preparing the base to incorporating flavorful add-ins, contributes to the overall success of the popsicle-making process. From selecting the right ingredients to perfecting the freezing process, this chapter delves into the essential techniques that elevate homemade popsicles from simple frozen treats to culinary masterpieces.

LAYERING THE POPSICLE INGREDIENTS

Mastering the art of layering introduces a dimension of complexity and delight that elevates these frozen treats to a culinary masterpiece. This chapter is dedicated to unraveling the secrets behind crafting popsicles that are not only visually captivating but also an explosion of diverse and harmonious flavors.

Lay the Base

The foundation of any exceptional popsicle lies in the carefully chosen base. Whether it's a refreshing fruit puree, a creamy yogurt blend, or a coconut milk infusion, the first layer sets the stage for the entire frozen symphony. This section delves into the nuances of selecting and preparing the perfect base, ensuring that each layer contributes a distinct element to the overall taste experience.

Sweeten It Up

Sweetness is the melody that ties the layers together, and in this segment, we explore the myriad options for sweetening your popsicle creation. From natural sweeteners like honey and maple syrup to the unique depth of flavor provided by agave nectar, discover the art of balancing sweetness to enhance overall enjoyment. This layer is where the popsicle transforms from a mere frozen treat into a sublime dessert experience.

Get Boozy

For those looking to add a touch of sophistication to their frozen creations, this section explores the world of popsicles. From fruit cocktails on a stick, learn the art of incorporating spirits into your popsicle repertoire. Navigate the delicate balance while maintaining the integrity of the flavors, unlocking a new realm of popsicle enjoyment for the more adventurous palate. Elevate your popsicle-making skills as we delve into the intricacies of each layer, ensuring that every bite is a sensory delight and a celebration of creative culinary expression.

FREEZING THE POPSICLES

The art of freezing is where the alchemy of ingredients transforms into the frozen delights we eagerly anticipate. Let's dive into the crucial elements that ensure your popsicles emerge from the freezer as perfectly frozen masterpieces, ready to tantalize taste buds.

Allow room for Expansion

The freezing process is a critical juncture in the creation of perfect popsicles, and understanding the dynamics of expansion is paramount to achieving frozen delights with flawless texture and appearance. As liquids transform into solids during freezing, they undergo expansion. Without ample room, the expanding liquid may push against the mold walls, causing deformation and uneven freezing. This can result in popsicles that are less visually appealing and may even impact their overall texture.

Crooked Sticks

The journey from liquid to frozen popsicle involves more than just the choice of flavors and ingredients; it also requires meticulous attention to the positioning of popsicle sticks during the freezing process. Crooked sticks can result from a variety of factors, with one primary contributor being the initial placement of the sticks. When inserting sticks into the liquid popsicle mixture, it's crucial to ensure they are centered and straight. Any deviation from the centerline can lead to an uneven distribution of freezing liquid, causing the sticks to set at an angle.

Regularly checking the popsicles as they freeze allows you to make adjustments if any sticks appear to be deviating from the desired position. By addressing these factors, you can significantly reduce the likelihood of crooked sticks, resulting in aesthetically pleasing and evenly frozen popsicles every time.

Freeze Time

The art of freezing popsicles is a delicate balance of time and temperature, ensuring the transformation from liquid concoction to frozen delight is executed with precision. Freezing time plays a pivotal role in achieving the ideal texture, flavor retention, and overall popsicle experience. The optimal freezing time for popsicles depends on various factors, including the size and composition of the popsicle mixture, the temperature of the freezer, and the desired texture. Generally, popsicles require several hours in the freezer to achieve a solid, yet not overly hard, consistency. Most recipes recommend a freezing time between 4 to 6 hours. Thicker molds may require more time for the center of the popsicle to solidify completely.

Freezing Speed

The freezing speed of popsicles is a crucial factor in determining the texture, consistency, and overall quality of the frozen treats. The speed at which popsicles freeze directly influences their texture. Slow freezing allows ice crystals to form gradually, resulting in a smoother and creamier texture. On the other hand, rapid freezing can create smaller ice crystals, contributing to a denser and icier consistency. Striking the right balance between these extremes is key to achieving the desired texture. Freezing speed also plays a role in preserving the flavor profile of the popsicles. Slow freezing allows the flavors to meld and develop, creating a more harmonious taste.

UNMOLDING THE FROZEN DELIGHTS

The final step in the popsicle-making journey is the delicate process of unmolding. From traditional molds to innovative designs, here's a comprehensive guide on unmolding popsicles.

The first consideration in unmolding is the choice of popsicle mold. Silicone molds, often preferred for their flexibility, ease the removal process. However, classic plastic molds and specialty shapes require specific techniques to prevent breakage.

Timing is everything when it comes to unmolding popsicles. Allowing them to freeze completely is crucial for maintaining their shape during removal. The recommended freezing time varies based on the size and ingredients of the popsicles. A gentle jiggle or visual inspection can indicate whether they are ready for the unmolding process.

The magic of warm water comes into play during unmolding. Running the mold under warm water for a few seconds helps loosen the popsicles, creating a slight separation between the frozen treat and the mold. This technique is particularly effective with plastic molds, where the heat facilitates a clean release.

Unmolding requires patience and precision. Rushing the process may lead to cracks or breakage. Gently wiggling the popsicle stick while applying consistent, light pressure aids in a smooth release. It's a delicate dance between anticipation and careful execution.

STORING THE POPSICLES

Proper storage is key to preserving the freshness and flavor of popsicles. Whether preparing a batch in advance or saving leftovers for later enjoyment, understanding the ins and outs of popsicle storage ensures a delightful frozen treat every time.

Individual Wrapping

For popsicles prepared in advance, individual wrapping is a smart choice. Using plastic wrap or parchment paper, wrap each popsicle separately before placing them in an airtight container. This prevents freezer burn, maintains flavor integrity, and allows for easy, on-the-go access.

Layered Storage

Layered storage is an efficient method for storing multiple popsicles in a single container. Separating layers with parchment paper or silicone sheets prevents them from sticking together. This organized approach makes it convenient to grab one popsicle without disturbing the others.

Freezer-Friendly Containers

Investing in freezer-friendly containers designed for popsicle storage ensures optimal conditions. These containers are designed to resist odors and freezer burn, preserving the original taste. Additionally, they often come with secure lids to safeguard against potential contamination.

Refreshing Leftovers

Revitalizing leftover popsicles involves strategic storage. Placing them in the freezer alongside a bowl of ice helps maintain a consistently cold environment, preventing premature melting. This simple trick ensures that even the last popsicle retrieved retains its refreshing allure.

These techniques ensure that each popsicle delights the senses, delivering a burst of flavor and satisfaction.

HOW TO CREATE LAYERS

Creating visually appealing and flavorful layers in popsicles elevates their aesthetic and taste. Whether aiming for distinct, clean layers or a harmonious blend of flavors, mastering the art of layering adds an extra dimension to these frozen delights.

Clean Layers

Achieving clean, defined layers in popsicles requires precision and a steady hand. Follow these steps for pristine, visually appealing results:

Gradual Freezing

Begin by pouring the first layer of liquid into the mold. Allow it to freeze partially, achieving a slushy consistency. This initial semi-frozen state helps create a clear boundary between layers, preventing unwanted blending.

Tilt And Pour

Tilting the mold at a slight angle, carefully pour the next layer over the partially frozen one. This controlled pouring minimizes disturbance to the lower layer, ensuring a clean separation. Use a spoon or spatula to guide the liquid for added precision.

Patience Is Key

After pouring each layer, patience is key. Allowing ample time for the liquid to freeze before adding the next layer prevents mixing and maintains distinct boundaries. This step-by-step approach contributes to the creation of visually striking, clean layers.

Blended Layers

For those seeking a more integrated and varied flavor experience, blended layers offer a dynamic and enticing alternative. Here's how to achieve perfectly blended layers in your popsicles:

Complementary Flavors

Select flavors that complement each other to create a harmonious blend. Consider combinations like strawberry and banana or mango and coconut for a balanced taste profile.

Simultaneous Pouring

Rather than waiting for each layer to freeze individually, opt for simultaneous pouring. Pour different flavored liquids into the mold at the same time, allowing them to naturally blend and intertwine. This approach creates a visually appealing and seamlessly integrated final product.

Swirling Techniques

To enhance the blending effect, experiment with swirling techniques. Use a thin utensil, like a skewer or toothpick, to gently swirl the different layers together. This adds an artistic touch and ensures a consistent flavor experience in every bite.

Popsicle Health Considerations

As the allure of homemade popsicles continues to captivate taste buds, it's essential to delve into the health considerations associated with these frozen treats. While popsicles offer a refreshing and delightful experience, understanding the impact on health allows for a mindful and balanced approach to consumption.

NUTRITIONAL BENEFITS OF HOMEMADE POPSICLE

Discovering the nutritional benefits of homemade popsicles unveils a delightful journey of flavor and wellness. In contrast to store-bought varieties laden with artificial additives, homemade popsicles provide a canvas for incorporating fresh fruits and nutrient-rich ingredients, elevating the frozen treat into a health-conscious delight.

Incorporating Fresh Fruits and Nutrient-Rich Ingredients

One of the key nutritional advantages of crafting popsicles at home lies in the freedom to embrace an array of fresh fruits and nutrient-dense components. From vibrant berries bursting with antioxidants to vitamin-rich citrus fruits, the possibilities are endless. These natural ingredients not only infuse popsicles with delicious flavors but also contribute essential vitamins, minerals, and antioxidants. By opting for whole and minimally processed elements, homemade popsicles become a wholesome treat that supports overall well-being.

Additionally, the versatility of homemade popsicles extends to including nutrient-rich bases like yogurt, coconut milk, or nut butter. These additions not only enhance the creaminess of the popsicles but also provide essential proteins, healthy fats, and probiotics, promoting a more balanced nutritional profile.

Dietary Considerations for Various Lifestyles

Homemade popsicles cater to diverse dietary preferences and lifestyles, making them an inclusive choice for everyone. For those following specific diets, such as vegan, gluten-free, or paleo, crafting popsicles at home allows for creative adaptations. Substituting traditional dairy with plant-based alternatives or choosing gluten-free sweeteners ensures that popsicles align with various dietary needs.

Furthermore, homemade popsicles offer a customizable approach to sweetness. By controlling the amount and type of sweeteners used, individuals can tailor popsicles to suit their taste preferences and health goals. This flexibility empowers individuals to indulge in a frozen treat without compromising on their dietary principles.

MANAGING SUGAR CONTENT

Embarking on the journey of crafting homemade popsicles entails not only a delightful exploration of flavors but also a mindful consideration of sugar content. The main art of managing sugar content, unraveling the possibilities of incorporating natural sweeteners, and creating low-sugar and sugar-free options to align frozen treats with individual preferences and health-conscious choices.

Natural Sweeteners and Sugar Alternatives

Elevating the sweetness of homemade popsicles involves a careful selection of natural sweeteners and sugar alternatives. Exploring beyond conventional white sugar, this section introduces a spectrum of choices like honey, maple syrup, agave nectar, and stevia. Each sweetener brings its unique flavor profile, allowing for a nuanced and personalized touch to the popsicle recipe.

Natural sweeteners not only contribute sweetness but also add additional nutrients and antioxidants to the mix. Honey, for instance, brings a rich taste while boasting antimicrobial properties, and maple syrup imparts a distinct earthy sweetness along with minerals like manganese and zinc.

Creating Low-Sugar and Sugar-Free Options

For those mindful of their sugar intake, the chapter further explores the realm of creating low-sugar and sugar-free popsicle options. Strategies such as using ripe fruits, which naturally contain sugars, allow for a reduction in added sweeteners without compromising on flavor. Additionally, the incorporation of sugar substitutes like erythritol, xylitol, or monk fruit sweetener provides alternatives for those seeking a sugar-free experience. By understanding the role of sugar in texture, freezing, and flavor enhancement, individuals can make conscious adjustments without sacrificing the essence of this frozen delight.

Popsicles: A Special Treat for Pets

Introducing a delightful twist to the world of frozen treats, this chapter explores the realm of popsicles crafted specifically for our furry companions. Our pets hold a special place in our hearts, and sharing a cool, tasty popsicle with them can be a bonding experience filled with joy and tail wags. This chapter unravels the art of creating popsicles tailored to the unique preferences and dietary needs of our beloved pets.

The Joy of Treating Furry Companions

The companionship of pets is a source of constant joy, and what better way to celebrate that bond than by sharing a popsicle? Whether it's a dog eagerly lapping up a fruity concoction or a cat savoring a fish-flavored frozen delight, the sheer happiness and excitement radiating from our pets create a heartwarming experience.

Understanding the preferences of different pets adds a personalized touch to the popsicle-sharing ritual. Dogs may relish the crunch of frozen fruits, while small animals like rabbits and guinea pigs may delight in icy vegetable treats.

Creating Safe and Delicious Pet Treats

Popsicles aren't just a refreshing delight for humans; they can also be a special treat for our furry friends. Crafting safe and delicious popsicles for pets involves a thoughtful selection of ingredients and a keen understanding of their unique dietary needs. The foundation of safe pet popsicles lies in the choice of ingredients. Opting for pet-friendly foods such as plain yogurt, unsalted peanut butter, or pet-safe broth ensures a treat that is both palatable and safe. Avoid ingredients like xylitol, chocolate, or artificial sweeteners, as these can be harmful to pets. This section delves into the specifics of selecting ingredients that cater to the nutritional requirements of different animals.

The joy of treating our pets to popsicles goes beyond a simple frozen treat. It symbolizes the shared moments of happiness and companionship that make the relationship between pets and their owners truly special. By understanding their preferences and ensuring the safety of the treats, this chapter encourages pet owners to indulge their furry friends in a delightful and safe popsicle experience.

Popsicles Adventures Around the World

Popsicles, a universally cherished frozen delight, have embarked on a global journey, captivating taste buds across continents with diverse flavors and cultural twists. This chapter unfolds a tantalizing exploration of popsicle variations from different corners of the world, showcasing the creativity and unique preferences that each culture brings to this frozen treat.

Japan's Mochi Pops

In the Land of the Rising Sun, popsicles take on a unique form with the introduction of Mochi Pops. These delightful treats feature a chewy rice cake exterior enveloping various ice cream flavors. The combination of the soft, sticky mochi texture and the cold, creamy ice cream creates a harmonious contrast that has become a favorite among those seeking a distinctive frozen experience.

Italy's Gelato on a Stick

Italy, known for its rich gelato tradition, introduces a twist to the popsicle scene with Gelato on a Stick. These popsicles capture the essence of authentic Italian gelato, offering a creamy, indulgent experience with flavors ranging from classic pistachio to sophisticated tiramisu. The artistry of Italian gelato craftsmanship is translated into a convenient and portable frozen treat.

Mexico's Paleta Paradise

South of the border, Mexico reigns as the kingdom of paletas, a vibrant and diverse array of popsicles made from fresh fruits, spices, and even chili. From the sweet and tangy Tamarind to the refreshing cucumber lime, Mexican paletas showcase a kaleidoscope of flavors that reflect the country's culinary richness. These popsicles bring a fiesta of taste to the streets, enchanting locals and tourists alike.

Thailand's Coconut Ice Pops

In the tropical paradise of Thailand, Coconut Ice Pops stand out as a cool and refreshing delicacy. Crafted from coconut milk and adorned with coconut shavings, these popsicles offer a taste of the exotic. Whether enjoyed on the bustling streets of Bangkok or the serene beaches of Phuket, Coconut Ice Pops encapsulates the essence of Thailand's tropical allure.

India's Kulfi Sticks

The Indian subcontinent introduces the world to Kulfi Sticks, a traditional frozen dessert with roots dating back to ancient times. Infused with aromatic spices such as cardamom, saffron, and pistachios, Kulfi Sticks deliver an indulgent experience that pays homage to India's rich culinary heritage. These popsicles are often sold by street vendors, adding to the sensory tapestry of bustling Indian markets.

United States Gourmet Pops

Across the United States, the popsicle landscape has evolved into a realm of gourmet creations. Artisanal popsicle shops offer an eclectic assortment of flavors, from Lavender Lemonade to Avocado Mint Chip. These gourmet popsicles often incorporate locally sourced ingredients, emphasizing a farm-to-stick ethos that resonates with the contemporary food movement.

Conclusion

As we reach the final chapter of this popsicle journey, it's time to savor the sweet memories and celebrate the artistry and joy that popsicles bring to our lives. From the humble beginnings of frozen juice on a stick to the intricate, flavor-infused creations we've explored together, popsicles have proven to be more than just a refreshing treat; they're a canvas for creativity and a source of unbridled joy.

Celebrating the Art and Joy of Popsicles

Popsicles are not just frozen desserts; they're edible masterpieces that captivate our senses. Throughout this book, we've dived into the world of popsicle artistry, exploring the myriad colors, flavors, and textures that can be achieved with a simple frozen stick. From the nostalgia of childhood favorites to the sophistication of gourmet creations, popsicles have a unique ability to transport us to moments of pure delight.

As we celebrate the art of popsicles, let's not forget the joy they bring to people of all ages. Whether shared with friends on a summer day or savored alone in quiet contemplation, the simple act of enjoying a popsicle can evoke smiles, laughter, and a sense of carefree happiness. Popsicles have a remarkable way of turning ordinary moments into extraordinary memories, creating a shared experience that transcends generations.

Encouragement for Continued Popsicle Explorations and Creations

As we bid adieu to this popsicle odyssey, the journey of exploration and creation doesn't have to end. The world of popsicles is vast and ever evolving, with new flavors, techniques, and trends emerging constantly. I encourage you to continue your popsicle adventures, experimenting with flavors that intrigue you, trying out innovative molds, and sharing your frozen creations with friends and family.

Popsicle-making is not just a culinary endeavor; it's a form of self-expression. So, let your imagination run wild. Combine unexpected flavors, play with textures, and create popsicles that reflect your unique tastes and personality. Whether you're a novice or a seasoned popsicle enthusiast, there's always room for discoveries and delightful surprises in the world of frozen treats.

Let's raise our popsicles to the joy they bring and the limitless possibilities they offer. May your future popsicle endeavors be filled with creativity, deliciousness, and moments of pure, frozen bliss. Remember that each icy masterpiece is a celebration of your culinary journey—one that is as unique and delightful as the popsicles themselves. Cheers to the continued exploration of the frozen wonders that bring happiness one lick at a time!

Healthy
Popsicle
Recipes

BUTTERSCOTCH W/
Caramel from Scratch

The combination of butterscotch caramel flavor is out of this world. No one can resist it. The kids love it and so does the adults. It only takes a few ingredients to make this at home. Do not miss out on it!

Prep Time: 10 mins
Cook Time: 15 mins
Extra Time: 5 hrs
Total Time: 5 hrs 25 mins

Nutrition Facts

Servings Per Recipe:	8
Calories:	213.7
Calories from Fat	113 g
Total Fat	12.6 g
Saturated Fat	7.8 g
Cholesterol	42.8 mg
Sodium	107.1 mg
Total Carbohydrate	24 g
Dietary Fiber	0 g
Sugars	22.4 g
Protein	2 g

Ingredients

¾ C heavy whipping cream

¾ C dark brown sugar, packed

2 tbsp unsalted butter, at room temperature

¾ tsp vanilla extract

¼ tsp kosher salt (flaky, or to taste)

1 tbsp cornstarch

1 ½ C whole milk

Directions

1. In a pot, combine butter, brown sugar with cream. Bring the mix to a boil.
2. Simmer on low for 10 minutes. Stir time to time.
3. Add the cornstarch and combine. Add milk gradually and stir continuously.
4. Cook for 5 minutes. Take off the heat.
5. Mix in salt and vanilla and combine. Let it cool down for 10 minutes.
6. Add to the ice pop molds and freeze for 6 hours.

Sweetened
Condensed Double Coconut

The coconut flavored popsicles are pure joy. They taste very refreshing. It complements the vanilla flavor perfectly. Adding the half and half and condensed milk makes it creamier.

Prep Time: 5 mins
Extra Time: 6 hrs
Total Time: 6 hrs 5 mins

Nutrition Facts

Servings Per Recipe:	6
Calories:	547.1
Calories from Fat	235 g
Total Fat	26.2 g
Saturated Fat	21.6 g
Cholesterol	32.5 mg
Sodium	219 mg
Total Carbohydrate	73.8 g
Dietary Fiber	1.9 g
Sugars	69.9 g
Protein	7.5 g

Ingredients

1 (13 ounce) can coconut milk

1 (14 ounce) can sweetened condensed milk

2⁄3 C half-and-half

1⁄4 tsp salt

1⁄4 tsp pure vanilla extract

3⁄4 C unsweetened dried shredded coconut

Directions

1. In a blender, add the half and half with vanilla.
2. Pour in coconut milk and condense milk. Add salt. Blend for 1 minute.
3. Add the shredded coconut and Add to the ice pop molds and freeze for 6 hours.

THURSDAY NIGHTS
on Campus

 Prep Time: 30 mins
 Extra Time: 6 hrs
Total Time: 6 hrs 30 mins

This orange lime flavors ice pops are too good to miss out on. The aroma, the zesty flavor, the freshness, everything about this recipe will blow your mind.

Nutrition Facts

Servings Per Recipe:	1
Calories:	62.6
Calories from Fat	0 g
Total Fat	0.1 g
Saturated Fat	0 g
Cholesterol	0 mg
Sodium	2.4 mg
Total Carbohydrate	15.7 g
Dietary Fiber	0.1 g
Sugars	13.5 g
Protein	0.4 g

Ingredients

¾ C grapefruit juice, freshly squeezed

¾ C orange juice, freshly squeezed

¼ C lime juice, freshly squeezed

¼ C maple syrup

Directions

1. Squeeze out the juice from the fruits.
2. Combine in a bowl. Mix in the maple syrup.
3. Add to the ice pop molds and freeze for 6 hours.

Strawberry Strata w/ Lemonade

There is something about the combination of strawberries and lemon that always works. Adding some yogurt to it makes it more nutrition dense. The layered option is impressive for not only kids but also for adults.

Ingredients

Lemonade:

1 1/3 C low-fat yogurt, plain or 1 1/3 C vanilla

1/4 C fresh lemon juice

5 tbsp sugar

Strawberry Strata:

1 pint strawberry, cored and quartered

1/4 C sugar

2 tbsp water

1 tsp lemon juice

1 C plain yogurt

Prep Time: 20 mins
Extra Time: 6 hrs
Total Time: 6 hrs 20 mins

Nutrition Facts

Servings Per Recipe:	10
Calories:	92.1
Calories from Fat	12 g
Total Fat	1.4 g
Saturated Fat	0.8 g
Cholesterol	5.1 mg
Sodium	34.8 mg
Total Carbohydrate	17.9 g
Dietary Fiber	0.7 g
Sugars	16.6 g
Protein	2.8 g

Directions

1. In a pot, combine sugar and lemon juice and stir until the sugar dissolves.
2. Mix in the yogurt and combine. Chill for 1 hour.
3. In another pot, combine strawberries with sugar and water and bring the mix to a boil.
4. Simmer on low for 5 minutes. Add to a blender. Add in lemon juice. Blend for 1 minute.
5. Chill for 1 hour. Add yogurt to the strawberry mix and combine.
6. Assemble the ice pops in layers.
7. Add to the ice pop molds and freeze for 6 hours.

THE BIG DICED
Strawberry

Prep Time: 10 mins
Extra Time: 6 hrs
Total Time: 6 hrs 10 mins

Here is a simple strawberry flavored ice pops recipe with chunks of fresh strawberries in it. This fresh chunk gives these ice pops a different texture and flavor. Adding milk and yogurt to it makes it creamier.

Nutrition Facts

Servings Per Recipe:	6
Calories:	22.3
Calories from Fat	6 g
Total Fat	0.7 g
Saturated Fat	0.3 g
Cholesterol	2.1 mg
Sodium	7.9 mg
Total Carbohydrate	3.5 g
Dietary Fiber	0.7 g
Sugars	1.8 g
Protein	0.7 g

Ingredients

1 C strawberry, pureed

6 tbsp milk

1 (5 1/3 ounce) container Greek yogurt

4 tsp agave nectar

½ tsp vanilla extract

½ C strawberry, diced

Directions

1. Combine the milk with yogurt in a bowl.
2. Add in the agave, strawberry puree and vanilla. Combine.
3. Add the diced strawberries and combine.
4. Add to the ice pop molds and freeze for 6 hours.

Inside Grapefruit
Outside Watermelon

The combination of watermelon with grape fruits may seem unusual, the flavors are spot on in this recipe. The orange juice makes the ice pops more refreshing and packed with nutritional value. It only takes 3 ingredients to make this delicious ice pop.

Ingredients

1 seedless watermelon, small
2 red grapefruits, sweet ruby red preferred

2 oranges, large

 Prep Time: 30 mins
 Extra Time: 6 hrs
 Total Time: 6 hrs 30 mins

Nutrition Facts

Servings Per Recipe:	20
Calories:	84.3
Calories from Fat	3 g
Total Fat	0.4 g
Saturated Fat	0 g
Cholesterol	0 mg
Sodium	2.3 mg
Total Carbohydrate	21.2 g
Dietary Fiber	1.6 g
Sugars	16.9 g
Protein	1.7 g

Directions

1. Add the watermelon chunks into a blender and make it smooth.
2. Run through a sieve so pure juice comes out.
3. Do the same with oranges and grape fruit juice.
4. Combine all the juices.
5. Add to the ice pop molds and freeze for 6 hours.

RAW HONEY W/
Any Berry

Prep Time: 5 mins
Extra Time: 6 hrs
Total Time: 6 hrs 5 mins

Who can resist good berry ice pops? Adding avocado to it makes it creamier. The herbs add a lot of flavors and uniqueness to the ice pops. The yogurt also adds more nutritional value.

Ingredients

2 C whole milk plain yogurt

2 C frozen berries, thawed

1 avocado

½ C raw honey

1 ½ tsp vanilla extract

1 tsp herbs, powder (optional)

Nutrition Facts

Servings Per Recipe:	1
Calories:	96.5
Calories from Fat	34 g
Total Fat	3.8 g
Saturated Fat	1.2 g
Cholesterol	5.3 mg
Sodium	20.6 mg
Total Carbohydrate	15.1 g
Dietary Fiber	1.1 g
Sugars	13.8 g
Protein	1.8 g

Directions

1. Combine the vanilla with yogurt in a bowl. Add in the herb and mix.
2. Add avocado cubes with berries in a blender. Add honey and blend until smooth.
3. Combine with herb mixture.
4. Add to the ice pop molds and freeze for 6 hours.

Complex
Triple Coconut

Here is a simple coconut ice pop recipe with a very creamy texture. The ingredients used are simple and affordable. You can use honey or stevia instead or sugar to make it healthier.

Ingredients

1 (15 ounce) can coconut milk

1/2 C sugar

1 C ice cube

1/2 C heavy cream

1/2 C milk

1/4 tsp imitation coconut extract

2 tbsp unsweetened dried shredded coconut (optional)

🥣 Prep Time: 10 mins

🕐 Extra Time: 6 hrs

🕐 Total Time: 6 hrs 10 mins

Nutrition Facts

Servings Per Recipe:	12
Calories:	205.3
Calories from Fat	90 g
Total Fat	10.1 g
Saturated Fat	8.2 g
Cholesterol	15 mg
Sodium	22.8 mg
Total Carbohydrate	28.8 g
Dietary Fiber	0.1 g
Sugars	27.4 g
Protein	1 g

Directions

1. Drain water from coconut milk.
2. In a pan, combine sugar with coconut milk.
3. Stir well until sugar dissolves.
4. Add ice cubes to is and wait for the mix to cool down.
5. Mix in milk, coconut extract and heavy cream. Mix well.
6. Add to the ice pop molds and freeze for 6 hours.

MORNING MOCHA
from Scratch

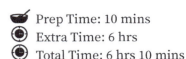 Prep Time: 10 mins

Extra Time: 6 hrs

Total Time: 6 hrs 10 mins

Who can resist a homemade mocha flavored ice pop? The half and half, makes the texture creamier. The coffee granules give it an aromatic flavor that will impress you.

Nutrition Facts

Servings Per Recipe:	10
Calories:	54.3
Calories from Fat	26 g
Total Fat	2.9 g
Saturated Fat	1.8 g
Cholesterol	8.9 mg
Sodium	26.9 mg
Total Carbohydrate	6.7 g
Dietary Fiber	0.4 g
Sugars	5.1 g
Protein	1 g

Ingredients

2 ½ C strong brewed coffee

4-5 tbsp sugar

2 tbsp unsweetened cocoa powder

1 pinch salt

1 C half-and-half

¼ tsp vanilla extract

Directions

1. In a bowl, combine sugar with hot coffee. Stir well.
2. Mix in salt and cocoa and combine. Heat for 2 minutes and mix well.
3. Add in vanilla and half and half. Combine.
4. Add to the ice pop molds and freeze for 6 hours.

Spicy Southwest
Cucumber Paletas

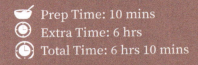

Prep Time: 10 mins
Extra Time: 6 hrs
Total Time: 6 hrs 10 mins

Have you ever tried cucumber ice pops before? This is definitely a unique flavor, but it will not hurt you to try this recipe. It is unique and very flavorful. The lime balances out the flavors.

Ingredients

2 large cucumbers, peeled and chopped (reserve about a 1/4 C)

1/4 C lime juice

1/4 - 1/2 jalapeno, finely chopped seeds removed (wear rubber gloves to protect your hands, and wash well afterward)

4 tbsp sugar

1/4 tsp salt

zest of two lime

Nutrition Facts

Servings Per Recipe:	1
Calories:	50.2
Calories from Fat	1 g
Total Fat	0.1 g
Saturated Fat	0 g
Cholesterol	0 mg
Sodium	99.2 mg
Total Carbohydrate	12.9 g
Dietary Fiber	0.6 g
Sugars	10.2 g
Protein	0.7 g

Directions

1. In a food processor, throw in the cucumbers with jalapenos.
2. Add salt, sugar, lime juice and blend into a smooth mix.
3. Add lime zest and chopped cucumber.
4. Add to the ice pop molds and freeze for 6 hours.

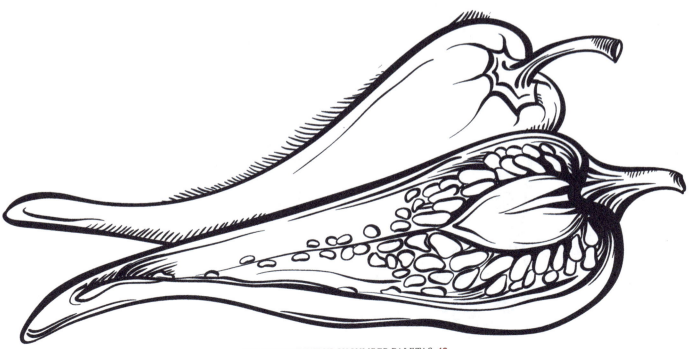

ZESTED
Graham Cracker

These simple lemon flavors milky ice pops are very delicious. It is authentic to the Mexican cuisine. Rolling them on crackers crumbs is optional but recommended for added crunch.

 Prep Time: 10 mins
Extra Time: 6 hrs
Total Time: 6 hrs 10 mins

Nutrition Facts

Servings Per Recipe:	6
Calories:	243.4
Calories from Fat	73 g
Total Fat	8.1 g
Saturated Fat	5.1 g
Cholesterol	29.9 mg
Sodium	118.4 mg
Total Carbohydrate	38.4 g
Dietary Fiber	0.1 g
Sugars	36.6 g
Protein	5.9 g

Ingredients

14 ounces sweetened condensed milk (not evaporated milk)

1/2 C half-and-half

1/2 C lemon juice (or lime juice)

2 tsp lemon zest (or lime zest)

1 pinch salt

2 C graham cracker crumbs, finely crushed (optional)

Directions

1. In a bowl, combine the half and half with condensed milk.
2. Add salt, zest and lime juice. Combine well.
3. Add to the ice pop molds and freeze for 6 hours.
4. Roll onto the crushed graham crackers before serving.

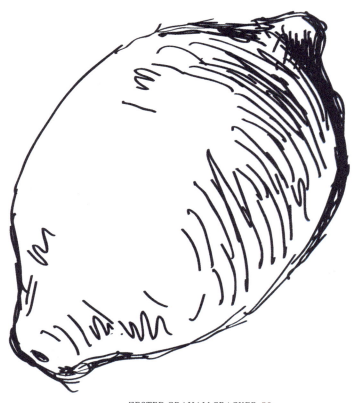

Rhubarb
Radiance

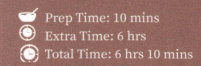

Prep Time: 10 mins
Extra Time: 6 hrs
Total Time: 6 hrs 10 mins

Nutrition Facts

Servings Per Recipe:	4
Calories:	226.7
Calories from Fat	23 g
Total Fat	2.6 g
Saturated Fat	1.4 g
Cholesterol	8 mg
Sodium	34.2 mg
Total Carbohydrate	50.1 g
Dietary Fiber	4.3 g
Sugars	43 g
Protein	3.9 g

Rhubarb ice pops has a distinct flavor that is loved by everyone. Combining it with strawberries only increases the flavors and the nutrition value of the recipe. Adding yogurt to it gives the ice pops a better texture.

Ingredients

1 lb rhubarb

2/3 C sugar

1 lb strawberry

1 C plain yogurt

Directions

1. In a pot, combine sugar with rhubarb. Cook for 10 minutes.
2. Add to a blender. Add in strawberries and yogurt.
3. Make it smooth and add to the ice pop molds and freeze for 6 hours.

MUNG BEAN
Pomegranate w/ Strawberries

Prep Time: 5 mins
Extra Time: 6 hrs
Total Time: 6 hrs 5 mins

You will love how unique and different this ice pop recipe is. Combining these beans with strawberries is a wonderful idea. The pomegranate juice also adds more flavor and nutrition value to the recipe.

Ingredients

1 C cooked adzuki beans

1 C coconut milk

1 C pomegranate juice

3 (1 g) packets stevia

6 ounces strawberries

Nutrition Facts

Servings Per Recipe:	6
Calories:	316.2
Calories from Fat	75 g
Total Fat	8.4 g
Saturated Fat	7.7 g
Cholesterol	0 mg
Sodium	23.4 mg
Total Carbohydrate	54.7 g
Dietary Fiber	4.9 g
Sugars	32.1 g
Protein	7.4 g

Directions

1. In a blender, add the beans with strawberries.
2. Pour in the juice, stevia and coconut milk.
3. Make it smooth.
4. Add to the ice pop molds and freeze for 6 hours.

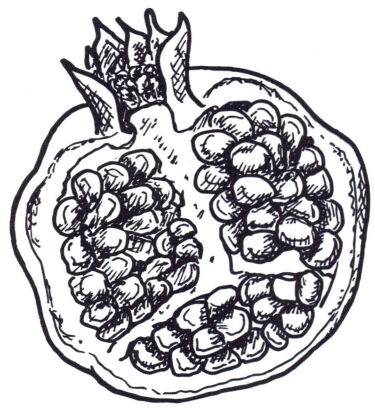

Coffee in the
Business District

Here is a delicious coffee flavored ice pop recipe with impeccable flavors. This recipe is authentic to the Vietnamese cuisine. The heavy cream and condensed milk add more flavor and creaminess to the recipe.

Ingredients

¾ C strong French roast coffee

2 C water, 200F

14 ounces sweetened condensed milk

1 C heavy cream

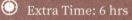
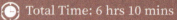

Prep Time: 10 mins

Extra Time: 6 hrs

Total Time: 6 hrs 10 mins

Nutrition Facts

Servings Per Recipe:	1
Calories:	2097
Calories from Fat	1103 g
Total Fat	122.6 g
Saturated Fat	76.6 g
Cholesterol	461 mg
Sodium	612.3 mg
Total Carbohydrate	222.6 g
Dietary Fiber	0 g
Sugars	216.2 g
Protein	36.5 g

Directions

1. In a pot, brew the coffee. Strain into a bowl.
2. Add condensed milk with heavy cream. Beat well.
3. Pour into ice pop molds.
4. Freeze for about 4 to 6 hours.

MR. BLUEBERRY
Meets Orange Juice

There is something about blueberry flavor that goes well with oranges. Adding vanilla yogurt to it makes it more delicious and creamier.

🥣 Prep Time: 5 mins
🕐 Cook Time: 10 mins
🕐 Extra Time: 4 hrs
🕐 Total Time: 4 hrs 15 mins

Nutrition Facts

Servings Per Recipe:	8
Calories:	59.8
Calories from Fat	10 g
Total Fat	1.1 g
Saturated Fat	0.7 g
Cholesterol	4 mg
Sodium	15.5 mg
Total Carbohydrate	11.8 g
Dietary Fiber	0.7 g
Sugars	10.2 g
Protein	1.4 g

Ingredients

1 1/2 C fresh blueberries

1 C water

1/2 C orange juice

3 tbsp sugar

1 C nonfat Greek vanilla yogurt

Directions

1. In a pot, combine blueberries with water and orange juice.
2. Add sugar and simmer on low for 10 minutes.
3. Let it cool down completely. Add to a blender and puree it.
4. Mix in yogurt and pour into ice pop molds. Freeze for about 4 to 6 hours.

Summery Citrus w/ Honeydew

Have you ever had honeydew ice pops before? They are very nutritious exotic fruit that has impeccable taste. Adding lime to it balances out the flavors perfectly.

Prep Time: 10 mins
Extra Time: 4 hrs
Total Time: 4 hrs 10 mins

Nutrition Facts

Servings Per Recipe:	10
Calories:	48.9
Calories from Fat	0 g
Total Fat	0.1 g
Saturated Fat	0 g
Cholesterol	0 mg
Sodium	13.3 mg
Total Carbohydrate	12.8 g
Dietary Fiber	0.6 g
Sugars	11 g
Protein	0.5 g

Ingredients

1/4 C sugar, super fine or granulated
1/4 C water

4 C honeydew melon, peeled, seeded and cut
2/3 C fresh lime juice

Directions

1. In a pot, combine sugar and water and dissolve it completely.
2. In a blender, add the honeydew melon with the lime juice.
3. Pour in the sugar syrup and make the mixture smooth.
4. Run it through a sieve.
5. Pour into ice pop molds.
6. Freeze for about 4 to 6 hours.

WHAT IS
Jungle Juice?

Here is a delicious and killer combination of apple juice, grapes juice and orange juice. If you can use freshly squeezed out juices, that will be best. But you can use the store-bought ones in this recipe too.

🥄 Prep Time: 10 mins
🕐 Extra Time: 4 hrs
🕐 Total Time: 4 hrs 10 mins

Ingredients

1 C apple juice

1 C orange juice

1 C grape juice

Nutrition Facts

Servings Per Recipe:	4
Calories:	94.4
Calories from Fat	2 g
Total Fat	0.3 g
Saturated Fat	0 g
Cholesterol	0 mg
Sodium	6.3 mg
Total Carbohydrate	22.8 g
Dietary Fiber	0.4 g
Sugars	20.1 g
Protein	0.7 g

Directions

1. Combine the juices in a jug.
2. Pour into ice pop molds.
3. Freeze for about 4 to 6 hours.

Honey Honeydew w/
Fresh Mint

The combination of blueberries with honeydew is a killer one. Adding honey to it makes it healthier and more nutritious. The lime flavor complements the blueberries and honeydew perfectly.

Prep Time: 15 mins
Extra Time: 4 hrs
Total Time: 4 hrs 15 mins

Nutrition Facts

Servings Per Recipe:	12
Calories:	59.8
Calories from Fat	2 g
Total Fat	0.2 g
Saturated Fat	0 g
Cholesterol	0 mg
Sodium	10.8 mg
Total Carbohydrate	15.5 g
Dietary Fiber	1.8 g
Sugars	12.2 g
Protein	0.7 g

Ingredients

½ honeydew melon
2 pints blueberries
1 lime
½ C water

2 tbsp honey
1 tbsp finely chopped of fresh mint

Directions

1. In a pot, combine mint, honey, water, and lime zest. Bring it to a boil and let it cool down.
2. In a blender, add blueberries, lime juice and honeydew chunks. Blend until smooth.
3. Strain the mixture. Combine it with the mint mixture.
4. Pour into ice pop molds.
5. Freeze for about 4 to 6 hours.

FLORIDA CREAM W/
Vanilla

Prep Time: 10 mins
Extra Time: 4 hrs
Total Time: 4 hrs 10 mins

The combination of orange juice with vanilla ice cream is pretty impressive. The texture becomes very creamy and the flavor outstanding.

Ingredients

1 (6 ounce) can frozen orange juice concentrate, softened juice, of your choice

1 (6 ounce) can water

1-8 ounce vanilla ice cream, softened

Nutrition Facts

Servings Per Recipe:	6
Calories:	66
Calories from Fat	5 g
Total Fat	0.6 g
Saturated Fat	0.3 g
Cholesterol	2.1 mg
Sodium	5.5 mg
Total Carbohydrate	14.7 g
Dietary Fiber	0.3 g
Sugars	14.3 g
Protein	1 g

Directions

1. In a blender, add the orange juice with vanilla ice cream.
2. Add water and blend until smooth.
3. Pour into ice pop molds. Freeze for about 4 to 6 hours.

Fresh
Mango

This mango flavored ice pop recipe is simple and flavorful. The star of the recipe is mangoes which you can find anywhere around the world during summer, you can use the frozen ones in this recipe too.

Ingredients

1 C drinking water
1 1/2 C ice cubes

1 C fresh mango, chopped
1/4 C sugar

Prep Time: 15 mins
Extra Time: 4 hrs
Total Time: 4 hrs 15 mins

Nutrition Facts

Servings Per Recipe:	10
Calories:	30.1
Calories from Fat	0 g
Total Fat	0 g
Saturated Fat	0 g
Cholesterol	0 mg
Sodium	1.2 mg
Total Carbohydrate	7.8 g
Dietary Fiber	0.3 g
Sugars	7.4 g
Protein	0.1 g

Directions

1. In a pot, bring the water to a boiling point.
2. Mix in sugar and simmer on low for 2 minutes.
3. Let it cool down. Add 2 C of ice cubes. Stir.
4. Add 2 tbsp mango into ice pop molds.
5. Pour in the water syrup.
6. Freeze for 4 hours.

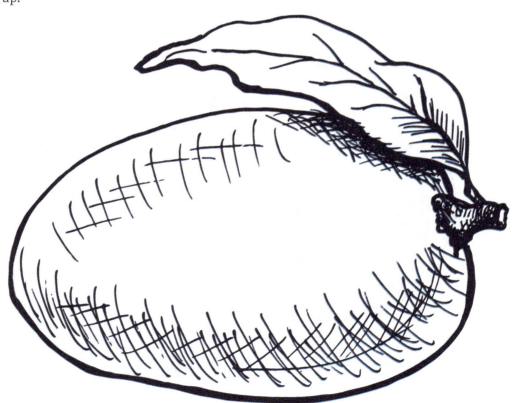

CALMING
Chamomile Peach Tea

 Prep Time: 20 mins
 Extra Time: 4 hrs
Total Time: 4 hrs 20 mins

A lot of flavors are going on in this ice pop recipe! There are two kinds peaches that are used. You can use only one if you can't find two where you live. The honey, the chamomile tea, and lemon, everything complements each other and create a wonderful flavor at the end.

Nutrition Facts

Servings Per Recipe:	10
Calories:	49.3
Calories from Fat	1 g
Total Fat	0.1 g
Saturated Fat	0 g
Cholesterol	0 mg
Sodium	14.9 mg
Total Carbohydrate	12.8 g
Dietary Fiber	0.9 g
Sugars	11.9 g
Protein	0.6 g

Ingredients

4 yellow peaches, ripe
2 white peaches, ripe
2 chamomile tea bags

1/4 C honey
1/2 small lemon, juice of
1 pinch kosher salt

Directions

1. In a blender, puree the peaches but keep 1/2 C peaches for later.
2. Chop the 1/2 C peaches.
3. Mix with honey, lemon juice, 2 tbsp chamomile tea leaves, and salt.
4. Fold in the chopped peaches.
5. Pour into ice pop molds.
6. Freeze for about 4 to 6 hours.

Gypsy Casino

The combination of orange flavored ice pops with yogurt vanilla flavor is pretty unique but it works. The kids love two different kinds of flavors or layers in their ice pops. They instantly gets amazed by those layers.

Ingredients

1/4 C orange juice

3/4 C low-fat plain yogurt

1/4 C white sugar

1/2 tsp vanilla

Directions

1. Add orange juice into the ice pop molds.
2. Freeze for 2 hours.
3. In a bowl, combine the yogurt with sugar and vanilla.
4. Pour into the molds.
5. Freeze for 3 hours.
6. Serve.

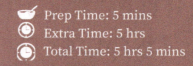

Prep Time: 5 mins

Extra Time: 5 hrs

Total Time: 5 hrs 5 mins

Nutrition Facts

Servings Per Recipe:	4
Calories:	103.7
Calories from Fat	4 g
Total Fat	0.5 g
Saturated Fat	0.3 g
Cholesterol	1.8 mg
Sodium	26.9 mg
Total Carbohydrate	22.9 g
Dietary Fiber	0 g
Sugars	22.6 g
Protein	2.1 g

LITTLE TANDIES W/
Raspberry

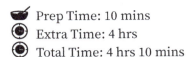 Prep Time: 10 mins
Extra Time: 4 hrs
Total Time: 4 hrs 10 mins

The combination of tangerine with raspberries is pretty unique and very delicious. It only takes two ingredients to make this summer ice pop recipe.

Ingredients

8 whole raspberries

16 ounces tangerine juice

8 toothpicks

Nutrition Facts

Servings Per Recipe:	4
Calories:	26.5
Calories from Fat	0 g
Total Fat	0.1 g
Saturated Fat	0 g
Cholesterol	0 mg
Sodium	0.1 mg
Total Carbohydrate	6.3 g
Dietary Fiber	0.8 g
Sugars	5 g
Protein	0.4 g

Directions

1. Stick a toothpick into each raspberry.
2. Add them to the ice pop mold.
3. Pour the tangerine juice into ice pop molds.
4. Freeze for about 4 to 6 hours.

Miami
After Dark

Who can resist a good orange ice pop that is very creamy in texture? Adding egg yolks to it changes the flavors and texture completely.

Ingredients

Sorbet:

1 C water
1/2 C sugar
2 C tangerine juice
1/4 C fresh lemon juice

Ice Cream:

1 1/2 C milk
2/3 C sugar
4 egg yolks
1/2 C sour cream

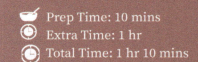

Prep Time: 10 mins
Extra Time: 1 hr
Total Time: 1 hr 10 mins

Nutrition Facts

Servings Per Recipe:	8
Calories	218
Total Fat	6 g
Saturated Fat	3 g
Carbohydrates	39 g
Dietary Fiber	0 g
Sugar	38 g
Protein	3 g
Cholesterol	85 mg
Sodium	32 mg

Directions

1. In a pot, combine sugar with water and bring to a boiling point.
2. Add the juices in a different bowl. Once the syrup cools down, mix in the juice.
3. Freeze for 4 hours.
4. To make ice cream, in a pot, combine 1/3 C sugar with milk. Bring to a boil.
5. Take off the heat. Once if cools down slightly.
6. Add 1/3 C sugar and combine.
7. Add egg yolks. Beat well. Heat on low for 5 minutes. Make it creamy in texture.
8. Strain it and then cool down. Mix sour cream and combine well.
9. Freeze for 6 hours. Assemble both and serve.

SEMISWEET CHOCOLATE W/
Buttery Bananas

These frozen bananas are super fancy with butter and chocolate chips. These popsicles are for the individual who loves their desserts dense. If you have yet to ever make a popsicle. Start here and get inspired.

Prep Time: 30 mins
Cook Time: 10 mins
Extra Time: 1 hr
Total Time: 1 hr 40 mins

Nutrition Facts

Servings Per Recipe:	8
Calories	323
Total Fat	18 g
Saturated Fat	11 g
Carbohydrates	47 g
Dietary Fiber	4 g
Sugar	36 g
Protein	3 g
Cholesterol	7 mg
Sodium	8 mg

Ingredients

8 medium bananas, peeled

8 wooden popsicle sticks

32 ounces semisweet chocolate, chopped or chips

4 tbsp unsalted butter

Directions

1. In a parchment paper, add the nuts, granola, jimmies, toasted coconut, crushed cookies, sprinkles and keep aside.
2. Cut the banana in half. Add popsicle sticks into each piece.
3. Freeze for 1 hour or longer.
4. Melt the chocolate with butter.
5. Dip the bananas in chocolate syrup.

Chipotle
Banana Pops

Banana popsicles are very convenient to make as they are readily available anywhere around the world and it is cost effective. Combining it with peanuts and chocolate syrup brings out impeccable flavors in the recipe.

Ingredients

5 bananas, just ripe
10 wooden popsicle sticks

1 C peanuts, finely chopped
3 C chocolate syrup, dark hard shell

Prep Time: 15 mins
Extra Time: 4 hrs
Total Time: 4 hrs 15 mins

Nutrition Facts

Servings Per Recipe:	10
Calories:	454.5
Calories from Fat	139 g
Total Fat	15.5 g
Saturated Fat	4.7 g
Cholesterol	0.9 mg
Sodium	318.8 mg
Total Carbohydrate	73.2 g
Dietary Fiber	5.3 g
Sugars	39.5 g
Protein	8.6 g

Directions

1. Cut the bananas in half width wise. Add popsicle sticks.
2. Coat the banana pieces into chocolate syrup.
3. Roll them in peanuts.
4. Freeze for about 4 hours or so.

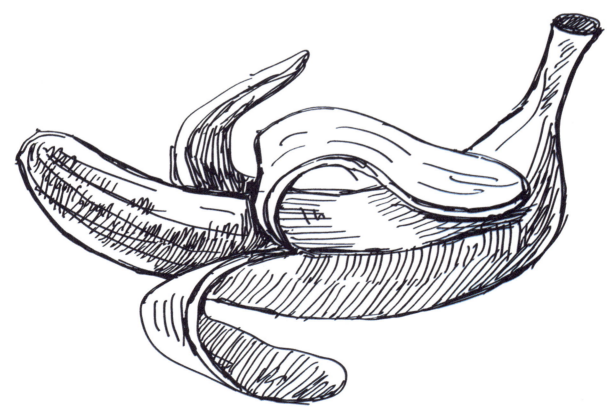

ANY BERRY
Blast

Here is a delicious berry yogurt ice pops recipe that is pretty delicious. Adding honey to it makes it healthier. You can combine different kinds of berries here or use just one berry too.

Nutrition Facts

Servings Per Recipe:	4
Calories:	69.3
Calories from Fat	17 g
Total Fat	2 g
Saturated Fat	1.3 g
Cholesterol	8 mg
Sodium	28.6 mg
Total Carbohydrate	11.5 g
Dietary Fiber	0 g
Sugars	11.5 g
Protein	2.2 g

Ingredients

1 C plain yogurt

1 C fresh fruit or 1 C frozen fruit, your choice of blueberries, strawberries, cherries, etc.

2 tbsp honey

4 wooden popsicle sticks or 4 plastic spoons

4 paper C, 5-ounce size aluminum foil

Directions

1. In a blender, throw in the berries with yogurt.
2. Blend until smooth and pour into paper C. Cover the top using foil.
3. Insert popsicle sticks in the middle freeze for 5 hours.

3-Ingredient
Strawberry

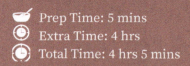

🥄 Prep Time: 5 mins
⏱ Extra Time: 4 hrs
🕐 Total Time: 4 hrs 5 mins

Here is a delicious strawberry ice pops that is made using simple ingredients but has massive flavor profiles. You can add some variation here If you want.

Ingredients

3⁄4 C fresh strawberries, hulled

1⁄4 C sugar

1⁄2 C water

Nutrition Facts

Servings Per Recipe:	8
Calories:	28.5
Calories from Fat	0 g
Total Fat	0 g
Saturated Fat	0 g
Cholesterol	0 mg
Sodium	0.6 mg
Total Carbohydrate	7.3 g
Dietary Fiber	0.3 g
Sugars	6.9 g
Protein	0.1 g

Directions

1. In a blender, add the strawberries with sugar.
2. Pour in the water. Blend until smooth.
3. Carefully pour into the mold and freeze for 4 hours.

MR. WATERMELON
Arrives for Summer

The combination of oranges with watermelon is pretty delicious. You can substitute the sugar with honey or stevia to make the recipe healthier.

🥣 Prep Time: 5 mins
🕐 Extra Time: 4 hrs
🕐 Total Time: 4 hrs 5 mins

Nutrition Facts

Servings Per Recipe:	1
Calories:	31.1
Calories from Fat	0 g
Total Fat	0.1 g
Saturated Fat	g
Cholesterol	0 mg
Sodium	0.8 mg
Total Carbohydrate	7.8 g
Dietary Fiber	0.1 g
Sugars	7.1 g
Protein	0.3 g

Ingredients

1 1⁄2 C diced watermelon
1 C orange juice

1 C water
1⁄4 C sugar

Directions

1. In a bowl, combine orange juice with sugar.
2. Stir well to dissolve the sugar.
3. Add water and watermelon in a blender.
4. Make it smooth. Combine with orange mixture.
5. Carefully pour into the mold and freeze for 4 h

Mango Harpies

Coconut flavor goes very well with mango flavors. Adding lime to it makes it more flavorful and refreshing. You can use stevia or honey instead of sugar.

Ingredients

1 ¼ C mangoes, chopped

¾ C coconut milk

1-2 tbsp sugar

1 tbsp lime juice

Prep Time: 5 mins
Extra Time: 4 hrs
Total Time: 4 hrs 5 mins

Nutrition Facts

Servings Per Recipe:	6
Calories:	161.5
Calories from Fat	55 g
Total Fat	6.2 g
Saturated Fat	5.8 g
Cholesterol	0 mg
Sodium	13.7 mg
Total Carbohydrate	27.1 g
Dietary Fiber	0.6 g
Sugars	25.9 g
Protein	0.7 g

Directions

1. In a blender, throw in the mangoes.
2. Pour in the coconut milk and lime juice.
3. Add the sugar and make it smooth.
4. Carefully pour into the mold and freeze for 4 hours.

PERFECT
for Picnics

Prep Time: 10 mins
Extra Time: 2 hrs
Total Time: 2 hrs 10 mins

If you want to fight a hot day of summer with a homemade ice pop, this recipe is just perfect for you. The combination of watermelon with oranges is a classic one, it never fails.

Nutrition Facts

Servings Per Recipe:	20
Calories:	28.5
Calories from Fat	0 g
Total Fat	0.1 g
Saturated Fat	0 g
Cholesterol	0 mg
Sodium	0.5 mg
Total Carbohydrate	7.2 g
Dietary Fiber	0.2 g
Sugars	6.5 g
Protein	0.3 g

Ingredients

5 C pureed watermelon (seedless)

3⁄4 C orange juice

1⁄3 C sugar

Directions

1. In a blender, add watermelon chunks.
2. Pour in the orange juice and add the sugar.
3. Blend until smooth. Carefully pour into the mold and freeze for 4 hours.

Woods
in Nebraska

Here is a simple strawberry lime ice pop recipe that is made with simple ingredients. It is perfect during a hot day of summer. Both kids and adults love this simple flavor.

Ingredients

1 C mashed strawberry
1/2 C water

3-4 tbsp sugar
juice of half lime

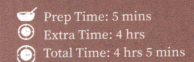

Prep Time: 5 mins
Extra Time: 4 hrs
Total Time: 4 hrs 5 mins

Nutrition Facts

Servings Per Recipe:	4
Calories:	48.1
Calories from Fat	0 g
Total Fat	0.1 g
Saturated Fat	0 g
Cholesterol	0 mg
Sodium	1.3 mg
Total Carbohydrate	12.2 g
Dietary Fiber	0.7 g
Sugars	11.2 g
Protein	0.2 g

Directions

1. In a blender, combine all the ingredients.
2. Make it smooth. Carefully pour into the mold and freeze for 4 hours.

PHILADELPHIA
Cookie

Prep Time: 15 mins
Extra Time: 4 hrs
Total Time: 4 hrs 15 mins

Who can resist a homemade Oreo flavored ice pop recipe? It is packed with flavors from the cream cheese and whipping cream. The texture is very creamy and delicious.

Nutrition Facts

Servings Per Recipe:	8
Calories:	247.8
Calories from Fat	168 g
Total Fat	18.7 g
Saturated Fat	10.5 g
Cholesterol	56.4 mg
Sodium	129.3 mg
Total Carbohydrate	19.1 g
Dietary Fiber	0.4 g
Sugars	13.7 g
Protein	2.3 g

Ingredients

4 ounces cream cheese (room temperature)
1/2 C confectioners' sugar

1 C heavy whipping cream
10 Oreo cookies

Directions

1. In a bowl, beat the cream cheese for 2 minutes.
2. Add sugar and beat well for 2 minutes. Add heavy cream and beat for 2 minutes.
3. Freeze for 45 minutes.
4. Divide the Oreos and process half of them and chop the other halves.
5. Add the chopped Oreos into the molds. Add the cream mix.
6. Freeze for 4 hours. Add the processed Oreos before serving.

Fat Free Chocolate w/ Strawberries

H ere is a delicious strawberry ice pop recipe that is suitable for people who are on a diet! This may sound weird but people on diet can have massive cravings for things like ice pops. This recipe will not give you calories but will fulfill your desires.

Ingredients

1 pint strawberry

1 pint fat free cream

low-fat chocolate

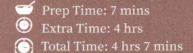

Prep Time: 7 mins

Extra Time: 4 hrs

Total Time: 4 hrs 7 mins

Nutrition Facts

Servings Per Recipe:	14
Calories:	28.6
Calories from Fat	5 g
Total Fat	0.6 g
Saturated Fat	0.3 g
Cholesterol	1.7 mg
Sodium	50 mg
Total Carbohydrate	5.1 g
Dietary Fiber	0.5 g
Sugars	2.9 g
Protein	1.1 g

Directions

1. In a blender, add the strawberry and puree it finely.
2. Combine it with cream and mix well.
3. Carefully pour into the mold and freeze for 4 hours.
4. Add melted low-fat chocolate before serving.

MEMORIES
of Samoa

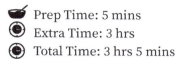
Prep Time: 5 mins
Extra Time: 3 hrs
Total Time: 3 hrs 5 mins

The combination of yogurt with pineapple juice Is pretty impressive. You can use any flavored yogurt here or plain yogurt will do too. You can use honey to make it healthier.

Ingredients

1 C vanilla yogurt

1 C pineapple juice

1 tsp sugar

Nutrition Facts

Servings Per Recipe:	8
Calories:	37.3
Calories from Fat	9 g
Total Fat	1 g
Saturated Fat	0.6 g
Cholesterol	4 mg
Sodium	14.7 mg
Total Carbohydrate	6 g
Dietary Fiber	0.1 g
Sugars	5.1 g
Protein	1.2 g

Directions

1. In a blender, add the vanilla yogurt.
2. Add pineapple juice and sugar.
3. Blend for 1 minute. Pour into molds.
4. Freeze for 3 hours.

Deluxe Granola
for Breakfast

This breakfast style popsicle is pretty unique and impressive. You can use any kind and any flavor granola here. The combination of yogurt with peanut butter is pretty delicious.

Ingredients

5 mashed bananas
2 C vanilla yogurt
1/2 C peanut butter

1 C sliced fresh fruit
1 C granola cereal

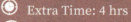

Prep Time: 20 mins
Extra Time: 4 hrs
Total Time: 4 hrs 20 mins

Nutrition Facts

Servings Per Recipe:	10
Calories:	217.9
Calories from Fat	100 g
Total Fat	11.2 g
Saturated Fat	2.9 g
Cholesterol	6.4 mg
Sodium	85.4 mg
Total Carbohydrate	24.8 g
Dietary Fiber	3.4 g
Sugars	13.1 g
Protein	7.4 g

Directions

1. In a bowl, combine the yogurt with peanut butter.
2. Add in the mashed banana and combine.
3. Add the sliced fruits into the molds.
4. Pour in 1/2 of the yogurt mixture.
5. Add the granola mix and the rest of the yogurt mix.
6. Freeze for 4 hours.
7. Serve.

CHICAGO CAFE
Coffee

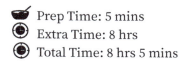
Prep Time: 5 mins
Extra Time: 8 hrs
Total Time: 8 hrs 5 mins

The combination of condensed milk with coffee is pretty delicious. The evaporated milk and vanilla improve the taste.

Nutrition Facts

Servings Per Recipe:	4
Calories:	152.4
Calories from Fat	57 g
Total Fat	6.4 g
Saturated Fat	3.9 g
Cholesterol	24.8 mg
Sodium	91.7 mg
Total Carbohydrate	17.5 g
Dietary Fiber	0 g
Sugars	10.5 g
Protein	6 g

Ingredients

1 C evaporated milk

2-3 tbsp instant coffee

1/4 C condensed milk

1 tsp vanilla extract

Directions

1. In a bowl, combine the condensed milk with evaporated milk.
2. Add in coffee and whisk well.
3. Add vanilla and combine.
4. Pour into the molds and freeze for 8 hours.
5. Serve.

Florida
Orange Juice

This simple popsicle recipe has impeccable flavors form banana and orange juice. You can add plain yogurt or any fruit flavored yogurt here.

Ingredients

½ C Florida orange juice
½ C yogurt (plain or flavored)

½ banana

Prep Time: 2 mins
Extra Time: 8 hrs
Total Time: 8 hrs 2 mins

Nutrition Facts

Servings Per Recipe:	6
Calories:	30.5
Calories from Fat	6 g
Total Fat	0.7 g
Saturated Fat	0.4 g
Cholesterol	2.6 mg
Sodium	9.7 mg
Total Carbohydrate	5.3 g
Dietary Fiber	0.3 g
Sugars	3.9 g
Protein	1 g

Directions

1. In a blender, add the orange juice with yogurt.
2. Add the banana and blend into a smooth mix
3. Add to the molds and freeze overnight.

SEATTLE COCONUT W/
Avocado

Prep Time: 20 mins
Extra Time: 5 hrs
Total Time: 5 hrs 20 mins

The combination of coconut with avocado is pretty impressive. The coconut flakes work like magic in this recipe. Using stevia or raw sugar makes it healthier.

Nutrition Facts

Servings Per Recipe:	12
Calories:	116
Calories from Fat	104 g
Total Fat	11.7 g
Saturated Fat	9.7 g
Cholesterol	0 mg
Sodium	16.3 mg
Total Carbohydrate	3.6 g
Dietary Fiber	0.6 g
Sugars	1.7 g
Protein	1.1 g

Ingredients

½ C fresh avocado

2 1/3 C unsweetened almond coconut milk

18 drops stevia or 5 tbsp raw sugar

½ C shredded sweetened flaked coconut

Directions

1. In a blender, add the avocado.
2. Pour in the milk. Add the coconut flakes, stevia, and blend for 1 minute.
3. Pour into the molds.
4. Freeze for 5 hours.

Mascarpone Cheesecake

This delicious cheesecake flavored popsicle is too good to miss out on. Adding raspberries and lemon juice improves the flavor.

Prep Time: 15 mins
Extra Time: 8 hrs
Total Time: 8 hrs 15 mins

Nutrition Facts

Servings Per Recipe:	10
Calories:	71.8
Calories from Fat	4 g
Total Fat	0.5 g
Saturated Fat	0.1 g
Cholesterol	0.6 mg
Sodium	39.6 mg
Total Carbohydrate	15.4 g
Dietary Fiber	1.2 g
Sugars	11 g
Protein	1.8 g

Ingredients

8 ounces mascarpone cheese
1/4 C fat free Greek yogurt
1 C skim milk
3 tbsp sugar

1/2 C graham cracker, crushed
1 C frozen raspberries
1 tsp lemon juice

Directions

1. In a bowl, beat the cheese with 2 tbsp sugar and milk. Add in yogurt and beat until creamy.
2. Fold the graham crackers gently.
3. In a blender, add the raspberries with sugar and lemon juice. Make it smooth.
4. Add the cheesecake mix. Combine. Pour into molds.
5. Freeze for 8 hours.

CONCORD
Raspberries w/ Kiwi

This layered raspberry and yogurt popsicle is impeccable. It is very easy to make too. The kiwi chunks give the popsicle a wonderful texture and flavor.

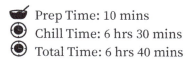

Prep Time: 10 mins
Chill Time: 6 hrs 30 mins
Total Time: 6 hrs 40 mins

Ingredients

2 kiwi fruits

1 C organic 100% concord grape juice

1 C plain yogurt, with fat

2 tsp torani sugar-free vanilla syrup

1 C raspberries

¼ - ½ C water

Nutrition Facts

Servings Per Recipe:	10
Calories:	44.9
Calories from Fat	8 g
Total Fat	1 g
Saturated Fat	0.5 g
Cholesterol	3.2 mg
Sodium	13.2 mg
Total Carbohydrate	8.4 g
Dietary Fiber	1.3 g
Sugars	6.5 g
Protein	1.2 g

Directions

1. Chop the kiwi. Add into the popsicle mold.
2. Combine 1/2 of yogurt with 1/2 vanilla and grape juice. Beat well.
3. Add to the molds. Freeze for 30 minutes.
4. In a blender add the raspberries, 1/4 C water and vanilla. Blend until smooth.
5. Add to the molds, add the kiwis, and freeze for 6 hours.
6. Serve.

Made in the USA
Las Vegas, NV
23 July 2024